FIELD GUIDE TO EGMONT KEY SNORKELING & DIVING

ANTHONY CHACOUR

Copyright © 2012 by Anthony Chacour

All rights reserved

Book printed in the United States of America

ISBN-13: 978-1478175117

This book is dedicated to my incredible parents

Contents

About This Book /References/ Note......................1

Snorkeling and Diving on Egmont Key......................2

About Egmont Key......................3

Fishes......................4

Ascidians......................36

Echinoderms......................41

Crustaceans......................45

Mollusks......................51

Cnidarians......................64

Sponges......................71

Algae......................78

Species Seen......................83

About This Book

In *Field Guide to Egmont Key Snorkeling & Diving*, one can find the photographs and information on 74 species of animals and algae. All the photographs in this book were taken by the author in the waters off Egmont Key. Under the photograph on the species pages is some information on the species. This information includes its common and scientific name, range, habitat, size, diet, and a miscellaneous fact.

References and Further Reading

Humann, P., and N. Deloach. 1989. Reef Fish Identification - Florida, Caribbean, Bahamas. New World Publications, Inc., Jacksonville, FL.

Humann, P., and N. Deloach. 1992. Reef Creature Identification - Florida, Caribbean, Bahamas. New World Publications, Inc., Jacksonville, FL.

Humann, P., and N. Deloach. 1992. Reef Coral Identification - Florida, Caribbean, Bahamas. New World Publications, Inc., Jacksonville, FL.

Kells, V., and K. Carpenter. 2011. A Field Guide to Coastal Fishes. The Johns Hopkins University Press., Baltimore MD.

Rehder, H., 1981. National Audubon Society - Field Guide to Shells. Alfred A. Knopf., New York.

Smith, C.L. 1997. National Audubon Society - Field Guide to Tropical Marine Fishes. Alfred A. Knopf., New York.

Egmont Key Alliance. < http://egmontkey.info/ >.

Florida Museum of Natural History. Ichthyology. < http://www.flmnh.ufl.edu/fish/ >.

Friends of Tampa Bay National Wildlife Refuges. < http://www.tampabayrefuges.org/ >.

Save Egmont Key. < http://saveegmontkey.com/ >.

Note

All the organisms in this book were identified visually. The author is solely responsible for any misidentifications.

Snorkeling and Diving on Egmont Key

The underwater world is unique, interesting, and beautiful. It is in this environment that we land adapted humans will find the organisms that are the most alien to us. This is perhaps why so many people are drawn there. For those that have the thirst to explore the underwater world, there are two primary methods to do so. These are snorkeling and scuba diving.

Snorkeling is a popular activity enjoyed by many people around the world. It is rather simple and anyone, who is at least moderately comfortable in the water, will be able to snorkel. Snorkeling does not require the expensive and cumbersome equipment needed for scuba diving. It also does not require scuba diving's intensive training. For these reasons snorkeling has served as an introduction to underwater exploration for many people.

Snorkeling can be done in any shallow water, however, the best snorkeling is found where there is structure or a reef. It is in these areas that the majority of fish and invertebrates tend to congregate.

The waters around Egmont Key provide perhaps the best opportunity for snorkeling in the Tampa Bay area. Most snorkeling on Egmont Key is done around a reef composed of the submerged ruins of Fort Dade. Specifically the Battery Henry Burchsted and Battery John Page. The reef is located off the southwest shore of the island. It is a few hundred yards offshore, in approximately 10 feet of water.

Even though it is shallow, scuba divers should not overlook the reef as a diving destination. The ruins of Fort Dade provide an array of holes and tunnels that can only be fully explored by scuba diving. It is in these areas that one can find some of the more cryptic creatures that inhabit the reef.

Over the years a diverse number of organisms have colonized the ruins. A few of these call the reef their permanent home. Some others, especially species of fish, are transient. They either reside there during certain times of the year or they simply pass by momentarily.

The reef at Egmont Key.

About Egmont Key

Egmont Key is a small island that occupies an area of around 400 acres at the mouth of Tampa Bay. It is part of the Florida State Parks system. The west shore of the island faces the Gulf of Mexico, with the east shore facing Tampa Bay. Egmont Key is only accessible by boat. Despite this limited accessibility, Egmont's natural attractions and history attract thousands of visitors a year. There are no concessions or other modern public amenities located on the island, however, there are several manmade structures.

Situated on Egmont Key are a lighthouse and the ruins of what was once Fort Dade. The 87 foot tall lighthouse is actually the second lighthouse to have called Egmont Key home. The first lighthouse was built in 1848. It was the second lighthouse to have been erected on the west coast of Florida. However, soon after its completion, a hurricane swept through the area and demolished the structure. The current lighthouse was then constructed ten years later.

Fort Dade began on Egmont Key in 1898. It was built in response to the threat posed by the Spanish-American War. Tampa at the time was beginning to grow and was gaining in importance as a community. Because of its increasing significance, Tampa required a fortification to protect it from potential attack. The attack never happened but Fort Dade continued to operate. It reached its peak in 1910 when it consisted of 70 buildings and housed a few hundred troops. A decade later it became apparent that Fort Dade was not needed any longer. The Army closed its doors in the early 1920's.

Egmont Key not only has historical significance but environmental as well. In fact much of the island was designated as a national wildlife refuge in 1974. Perhaps one of the better known inhabitants of the island is the Gopher Tortoise *(Gopherus polyphemus)*. The Gopher Tortoise is considered threatened and is federally protected by the U.S. Fish and Wildlife Service. Another reptile that can be found on Egmont Key is the endangered Loggerhead Sea Turtle *(Caretta caretta)*. During the Spring and early Summer, female Loggerhead turtles make their way to Egmont Key from open waters to lay their eggs on the beach.

Around 117 species of birds call Egmont Key home, whether permanently or temporarily. Among the species are the American Oystercatcher *(Haematopus palliates)*, Black Skimmer *(Rynchops niger)*, Brown Pelican *(Pelecanus occidentalis)*, Laughing Gull *(Leucophaeus atricilla)*, Royal Tern *(Thalasseus maximus)*, and Sandwich Tern *(Thalasseus sandvicensis)*. The area provides a safe refuge for birds to nest or rest during their migrations. The National Audubon Society considers Egmont Key a globally important bird area.

Erosion has taken its toll on Egmont Key throughout the years. Especially on the west side of the island. Around half of Egmont's land area has eroded away since the first survey was done in 1877. There are continuous efforts, such as beach replenishments, that take place to help stem the threat posed by erosion.

FISHES

Fish are perhaps the most familiar of aquatic animals. The fossil record for fish goes back over 500 million years. Today there are around 30,000 known species worldwide. They are extremely varied in their form and life histories. The smallest fish in the world is *Paedocypris progenetica*. It is found in Indonesia and at 0.31 inch long, it is the smallest vertebrate. The largest fish is the Whale Shark. It can reach a length of over 45 feet and weigh up to 36 tons. The Whale Shark can be found in the Gulf of Mexico.

Scaled Sardine
Harengula jaguana

Range: From the Northeastern U.S. to Florida and throughout the Gulf of Mexico to Brazil. Also found in the Caribbean.

Habitat: Inhabits bays, coastal areas, and open water.

Size: Up to a length of 6 inches.

Diet: Zooplankton.

Misc.: Scaled Sardines are a popular baitfish.

Gulf Toadfish
Opsanus beta

Range: South Florida and throughout the Gulf of Mexico.

Habitat: Inhabits hard bottom and seagrass up to depths of 800 feet.

Size: Up to a length of 12 inches.

Diet: Fishes and invertebrates.

Misc.: The Gulf Toadfish can survive for extended periods of time out of the water.

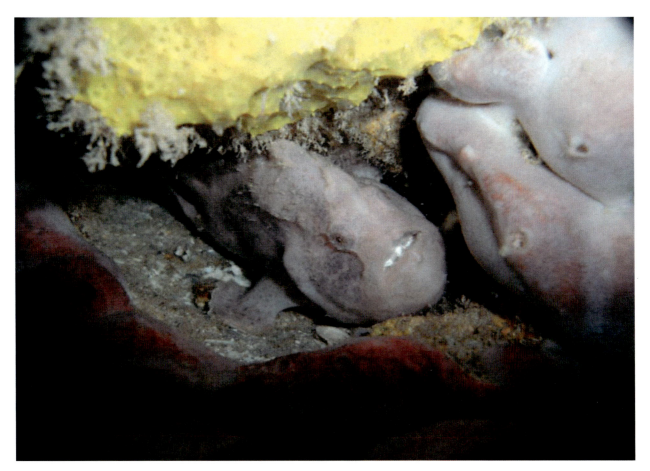

Ocellated Frogfish
Antennarius ocellatus

Range: From the Carolinas to the west coast of Florida. Also from the Yucatan Peninsula to northern South America and the Bahamas.

Habitat: Inhabits structure, sand, and soft bottom up to depths of 500 feet.

Size: Up to a length of 15 inches.

Diet: Fishes and crustaceans.

Misc.: The Ocellated Frogfish has the ability to change colors in order to camouflage with its surroundings.

Polka-Dot Batfish
Ogcocephalus cubifrons

Range: From the Carolinas to the Florida Panhandle. Also found in the Bahamas and southern Mexico.

Habitat: Inhabits sand, soft bottom, and seagrass up to depths of 230 feet.

Size: Up to a length of 15 inches.

Diet: Small fishes and invertebrates.

Misc.: The Polka-Dot Batfish is an ungainly swimmer and usually "crawls" along the bottom.

Atlantic Needlefish
Strongylura marina

Range: From New England to Florida and throughout the Gulf of Mexico to Brazil.

Habitat: Inhabits inshore waters. Usually right below the surface. It occasionally ventures into fresh water.

Size: Up to a length of 2 feet.

Diet: Small fishes and shrimp.

Misc.: The bones of the Atlantic Needlefish are green.

Barbfish
Scorpaena brasiliensis

Range: From the southern Atlantic coast of the U.S. to Florida and throughout the Gulf of Mexico to Brazil. Also found in the Caribbean.

Habitat: Inhabits many types of bottoms up to depths of 300 feet.

Size: Up to a length of 14 inches.

Diet: Fishes and crustaceans.

Misc.: The spines of the Barbfish are venomous.

Black Sea Bass
Centropristis striata

Range: From the Northeastern U.S. to both coasts of Florida.

Habitat: Inhabits structure, hard bottom, and reefs up to depths of 250 feet.

Size: Up to a length of 15 inches.

Diet: Small fishes and invertebrates.

Misc.: The Black Sea Bass is an important commercial and recreational species.

Sand Perch
Diplectrum formosum

Range: From the Carolinas to Florida and throughout the Gulf of Mexico to Uruguay. Also found in the Bahamas.

Habitat: Inhabits structure and sand bottom up to depths of 250 feet.

Size: Up to a length of 12 inches.

Diet: Small fishes and invertebrates.

Misc.: The Sand Perch is in the same family as Sea Basses and Groupers.

Red Grouper
Epinephelus morio

Range: From the Carolinas to Florida and throughout the Gulf of Mexico to Brazil. Also found in the Caribbean.

Habitat: Inhabits structure and soft bottom up to depths of 1000 feet.

Size: Up to a length of 4 feet and a weight of 50 pounds.

Diet: Fishes and invertebrates.

Misc.: The Red Grouper is an important commercial and recreational species. The one in the photo is a juvenile. Adult Red Grouper move to deeper water.

Gag Grouper
Mycteroperca microlepis

Range: From the Carolinas to Florida and throughout the Gulf of Mexico to the Yucatan Peninsula.

Habitat: Inhabits structure and reefs up to depths of 500 feet.

Size: Up to a length of over 4.5 feet and a weight of 80 pounds.

Diet: Fishes and crustaceans.

Misc.: The Gag Grouper is an important commercial and recreational species.

Whitespotted Soapfish
Rypticus maculatus

Range: From the Carolinas to Florida and throughout the Gulf of Mexico.

Habitat: Inhabits structure and reefs up to depths of 30 feet.

Size: Up to a length of 8 inches.

Diet: Small fishes and invertebrates.

Misc.: The Whitespotted Soapfish secretes a mucus that feels like soap.

Belted Sandfish
Serranus subligarius

Range: From the Carolinas to Florida and in the Gulf of Mexico to Texas.

Habitat: Inhabits structure and reefs up to depths of 60 feet.

Size: Up to a length of 4 inches.

Diet: Small fishes and invertebrates.

Misc.: Belted Sandfish are hermaphroditic.

Leatherjacket
Oligoplites saurus

Range: From southern New England to Florida and throughout the Gulf of Mexico to Brazil. Also found in the Caribbean.

Habitat: Inhabits shallow coastal waters and estuaries.

Size: Up to a length of 12 inches.

Diet: Small fishes and invertebrates.

Misc.: The Leatherjacket is sold commercially in some parts of its range.

Lookdown
Selene vomer

Range: From New England to Florida and throughout the Gulf of Mexico to Uruguay. Also found in Bermuda.

Habitat: Inhabits coastal waters up to depths of 30 feet.

Size: Up to a length of 12 inches.

Diet: Fishes and invertebrates.

Misc.: The Lookdown can be found in the aquarium trade.

Gray Snapper
Lutjanus griseus

Range: From southern New England to Florida and throughout the Gulf of Mexico to Brazil. Also found in Bermuda, Bahamas, and the Caribbean.

Habitat: Inhabits structure and reefs up to depths of 600 feet. It can occasionally be found in fresh water.

Size: Up to a length of 2 feet.

Diet: Fishes and invertebrates.

Misc.: Another name for the Gray Snapper is Mangrove Snapper. It is a popular game and food fish.

White Grunt
Haemulon plumierii

Range: From the Carolinas to Florida and throughout the Gulf of Mexico to Brazil. Also found in Bermuda, the Bahamas, and the Caribbean.

Habitat: Inhabits structure, reefs, and seagrass up to depths of 100 feet.

Size: Up to a length of 18 inches.

Diet: Small fishes and invertebrates.

Misc.: The White Grunt is a popular recreational and food fish.

Pigfish
Orthopristis chrysoptera

Range: From the Northeastern U.S. to Florida and throughout the Gulf of Mexico to the Yucatan Peninsula. Also found in Bermuda and the Bahamas.

Habitat: Inhabits structure, soft bottom, and seagrass up to depths of 70 feet.

Size: Up to a length of 15 inches.

Diet: Small fishes and invertebrates.

Misc.: The Pigfish is commonly used as a baitfish.

Sheepshead
Archosargus probatocephalus

Range: From southern Canada to Florida and throughout the Gulf of Mexico to Brazil.

Habitat: Inhabits structure and hard bottom up to depths of 40 feet.

Size: Up to a length of 29 inches.

Diet: Fishes and invertebrates.

Misc.: The Sheepshead is a popular game and food fish.

Spottail Pinfish
Diplodus holbrookii

Range: From the Northeastern U.S. to Florida and throughout the Gulf of Mexico.

Habitat: Inhabits hard bottom and seagrass up to depths of 40 feet.

Size: Up to a length of 12 inches.

Diet: Small invertebrates and vegetation.

Misc.: The Spottail Pinfish is often used for bait.

Pinfish

Lagodon rhomboides

Range: From southern New England to Florida and throughout the Gulf of Mexico to the Yucatan Peninsula.

Habitat: Inhabits structure and seagrass up to depths of 65 feet.

Size: Up to a length of 8 inches.

Diet: Small fishes, invertebrates, and vegetation.

Misc.: Pinfish are a popular baitfish.

Cubbyu
Pareques umbrosus

Range: From the Carolinas to Florida and throughout the Gulf of Mexico. Also found in Bermuda.

Habitat: Inhabits structure and reefs up to depths of 300 feet.

Size: Up to a length of 8 inches.

Diet: Invertebrates.

Misc.: Juveniles are silver with black horizontal stripes.

Spotfin Butterflyfish
Chaetodon ocellatus

Range: From New England to Florida and throughout the Gulf of Mexico. Also found in Bermuda, the Bahamas, and the Caribbean.

Habitat: Inhabits structure and reefs up to depths of 60 feet.

Size: Up to a length of 8 inches.

Diet: Invertebrates.

Misc.: The Spotfin Butterflyfish is popular in the aquarium trade.

Cocoa Damselfish
Stegastes variabilis

Range: From Florida to the northern Gulf of Mexico and from the Yucatan Peninsula to Brazil. Also found in the Bahamas and the Caribbean.

Habitat: Inhabits structure and reefs up to depths of 90 feet.

Size: Up to a length of 4.5 inches.

Diet: Invertebrates and algae.

Misc.: Juvenile Cocoa Damselfish are blue and yellow.

Slippery Dick
Halichoeres bivittatus

Range: From the Carolinas to Florida and throughout the Gulf of Mexico to Brazil. Also found in Bermuda, the Bahamas, and the Caribbean.

Habitat: Inhabits hard bottom and reefs up to depths of 40 feet.

Size: Up to a length of 7 inches.

Diet: Invertebrates.

Misc.: The Slippery Dick will go through three color phases as it gets larger.

Southern Stargazer
Astroscopus y-graecum

Range: From the Carolinas to Florida and throughout the Gulf of Mexico to northern South America.

Habitat: Inhabits sand and soft bottom up to depths of 230 feet.

Size: Up to a length of 22 inches.

Diet: Fishes.

Misc.: The Southern Stargazer can emit an electrical charge of up to 50 volts.

Zebratail Blenny
Hypleurochilus caudovittatus

Range: Gulf coast of Florida.

Habitat: Inhabits structure, reefs, and sand bottom in shallow water.

Size: Up to a length of 2.5 inches.

Diet: Small invertebrates and algae.

Misc.: The Zebratail Blenny was first described by science as a species in 1994. The specimen was taken from Egmont Key.

Seaweed Blenny
Parablennius marmoreus

Range: From the Northeastern U.S. to Florida and throughout the Gulf of Mexico to Brazil. Also found in Bermuda and the Bahamas.

Habitat: Inhabits structure and sand bottom up to depths of 30 feet.

Size: Up to a length of 3 inches.

Diet: Small invertebrates and algae.

Misc.: Popular in the aquarium trade and can be variety of colors.

Atlantic Spadefish
Chaetodipterus faber

Range: From New England to Florida and throughout the Gulf of Mexico to Brazil. Also found in Bermuda, the Bahamas, and the Caribbean.

Habitat: Inhabits structure and reefs up to depths of 70 feet.

Size: Up to a length of 3 feet.

Diet: Invertebrates.

Misc.: The Atlantic Spadefish is a popular recreational fish.

Spanish Mackeral
Scomberomorus maculatus

Range: From southern Canada to Florida and throughout the Gulf of Mexico. Also found in Bermuda.

Habitat: Inhabits inshore, nearshore, and open waters.

Size: Up to a length of 3 feet.

Diet: Small fishes and invertebrates such as squid and shrimp.

Misc.: The Spanish Mackeral is an important commercial and recreational species.

Scrawled Cowfish
Acanthostracion quadricornis

Range: From southern New England to Florida and throughout the Gulf of Mexico to Brazil. Also found in Bermuda and has been recorded off the coast of West Africa.

Habitat: Inhabits structure and seagrass up to depths of 250 feet.

Size: Up to a length of 22 inches.

Diet: Invertebrates and vegetation.

Misc.: The Scrawled Cowfish is popular in aquariums.

Bandtail Puffer
Sphoeroides spengleri

Range: From southern New England to Florida and throughout the Gulf of Mexico to Brazil.

Habitat: Inhabits structure and seagrass up to depths of 35 feet.

Size: Up to a length of 12 inches.

Diet: Invertebrates and vegetation.

Misc.: The skin and organs of the Bandtail Puffer contains a toxin.

Ascidians

Ascidians or tunicates are unique among invertebrates. That is because in their larval stage they are more similar to vertebrates. The larvae posses several vertebrate characteristics, including a notochord. The notochord is the precursor of the backbone in vertebrate animals. Ascidians eventually lose these characteristics. There are simple and compound ascidians. The compound ascidians are an assemblage of many small zooids found in a common test. There are over 2,000 known species.

Pleated Sea Squirt
Styela plicata

Range: From the Carolinas to Florida and throughout the Gulf of Mexico. Also found in the Caribbean.

Habitat: Inhabits structure and reefs up to depths of 100 feet.

Size: Up to a length of 3.5 inches.

Diet: Plankton that is filtered from the water.

Misc.: The Pleated Sea Squirt has been introduced to other areas of the world, where it is considered an invasive species.

Sea Liver
Eudistoma hepaticum

Range: The Southeast Atlantic coast of the U.S. and the Gulf of Mexico.

Habitat: Inhabits structure and reefs up to depths of 600 feet.

Size: Colony up to a width of over 12 inches.

Diet: Plankton that is filtered from the water.

Misc.: The Sea Liver is the most common ascidian found at Egmont Key. Unhealthy colonies may be light green or white in color.

Sea Pork
Aplidium stellatum

Range: From Canada to Florida and throughout the Gulf of Mexico.

Habitat: Inhabits structure and reefs up to depths of 150 feet.

Size: Colony up to a width of over 8 inches.

Diet: Plankton that is filtered from the water.

Misc.:   The Sea Pork gets its name due to its resemblance to raw pork when out of the water.

Lister's Encrusting Tunicate
Diplosoma listerianum

Range: Atlantic and Pacific coasts of North and South America. Also found in European waters.

Habitat: Inhabits structure and reefs up to depths of 250 feet.

Size: Colony up to a width of 8 inches.

Diet: Plankton that is filtered from the water.

Misc.: The Lister's Encrusting Tunicate is native to the waters of Northern Europe. It has colonized other areas by riding on the hulls of ships.

ECHINODERMS

The word echinoderm comes from the Greek word for "spiny skin". Some examples of echinoderms are sea urchins, starfish, and sea cucumbers. There are around 7,000 known species. Echinoderms arose around 540 million years ago. Their bodies posses radial symmetry. This means that the anatomical parts of the animal are arranged around its axis. Many echinoderms are able to regenerate missing body parts. Echinoderms are only found in marine environments. Some can be found in the deepest parts of the oceans.

Small-Spine Sea Star
Echinaster spinulosus

Range: From the Carolinas to Florida and throughout the Gulf of Mexico to Central America. Also found in the Caribbean.

Habitat: Inhabits hard and sand bottom up to depths of 130 feet.

Size: Up to a width of 6 inches.

Diet: Invertebrates.

Misc.: The Small-Spine Sea Star can be found in the aquarium trade.

Purple Sea Urchin
Arbacia punctulata

Range: From southern New England to Florida and throughout the Gulf of Mexico to the Yucatan Peninsula. Also found in the Caribbean.

Habitat: Inhabits structure and hard bottom up to depths of 750 feet.

Size: Body up to a diameter of 4 inches.

Diet: Algae.

Misc.: The Purple Sea Urchin is often used in medical research.

Variegated Urchin
Lytechinus variegatus

Range: From the Carolinas to Florida and throughout the Gulf of Mexico to Brazil. Also found in Bermuda, the Bahamas, and the Caribbean.

Habitat: Inhabits hard bottom, sand, and seagrass up to depths of 160 feet.

Size: Body up to a diameter of 3 inches.

Diet: Algae and seagrass.

Misc.: The Variegated Urchin often has bivalve shells and shell pieces stuck to its spines.

CRUSTACEANS

Crustaceans are invertebrates that belong to the phylum Arthropoda. Other Arthropods are insects and arachnids. Crustaceans include such animals as crabs, lobsters, and shrimp. Some characteristics of crustaceans are an external skeleton called an exoskeleton, a segmented body, and appendages that are jointed. There are around 42,000 known species. The largest of which is the Japanese Spider Crab. It can attain a leg span of 13 feet and a weight of 44 pounds.

Giant Hermit Crab
Petrochirus diogenes

Range: From the Carolinas to Florida and throughout the Gulf of Mexico to Brazil. Also found in the Caribbean.

Habitat: Inhabits sand and soft bottom near structure and reefs up to depths of 430 feet.

Size: Up to a length of 8 inches.

Diet: Invertebrates. Will sometimes kill and eat a gastropod before taking its shell.

Misc.: The Giant Hermit Crab is the largest hermit crab found in the waters of the Continental United States.

Dimpled Hermit Crab
Pagurus impressus

Range: From the Carolinas to Florida and throughout the Gulf of Mexico.

Habitat: Inhabits structure, sand bottom, and seagrass up to depths of 100 feet.

Size: Up to a length of 3 inches.

Diet: Invertebrates.

Misc.: Another common name for the Dimpled Hermit Crab is the Palmate Hermit Crab.

Florida Stone Crab
Menippe mercenaria

Range: From the Carolinas to Florida and throughout the Gulf of Mexico. Also found in the Bahamas.

Habitat: Inhabits reefs, sand, and soft bottom up to depths of 60 feet.

Size: Carapace up to a width of 6 inches.

Diet: Invertebrates and vegetation.

Misc.: The Florida Stone Crab supports an important fishery in Florida. Only the claws are harvested and the crab is released alive.

Coral Clinging Crab
Mithrax hispidus

Range: From the Northeastern U.S. to Florida and throughout the Gulf of Mexico to Brazil. Also found in the Caribbean.

Habitat: Inhabits structure and reefs up to depths of 50 feet.

Size: Carapace up to a width of 3 inches.

Diet: Scavenges and will also consume small invertebrates and vegetation.

Misc.: The Coral Clinging Crab can be found in the aquarium trade.

Yellowline Arrow Crab

Stenorhynchus seticornis

Range: Atlantic and Gulf coast of Florida. Also found in the Bahamas and the Caribbean.

Habitat: Inhabits structure and reefs up to depths of 130 feet.

Size: Carapace up to a length of 2.5 inches.

Diet: Scavenges and will also consume marine worms.

Misc.: The Yellowline Arrow Crab is a popular species in the aquarium trade.

MOLLUSKS

Mollusks are a diverse group of invertebrates. There are around 85,000 known species. Mollusks include such animals as oysters, clams, snails, octopuses, and squids. Octopuses and squids are considered to be the most intelligent of invertebrates. The largest mollusk and invertebrate in the world is the Colossal Squid, which is found in the cold waters around Antarctica. It can reach a length of over 45 feet and weigh over a ton.

Florida Fighting Conch
Strombus alatus

Range: From the Carolinas to Florida and throughout the Gulf of Mexico.

Habitat: Inhabits sand bottom and seagrass up to depths of 20 feet.

Size: Up to a length of 4 inches.

Diet: Algae.

Misc.: The Florida Fighting Conch in the photo is not a mature specimen.

Tinted Cantharus
Pisania tincta

Range: From the Carolinas to Florida and throughout the Gulf of Mexico to Brazil. Also found in Bermuda and the Caribbean.

Habitat: Inhabits reefs, hard bottom, and sand up to depths of 250 feet.

Size: Up to a length of 1.25 inches.

Diet: Small invertebrates.

Misc.: The Tinted Cantharus is sometimes found in the aquarium trade.

Lightning Whelk
Busycon contrarium

Range: Southeastern coast of the U.S. and the Gulf of Mexico to Texas.

Habitat: Inhabits sand and soft bottom up to depths of 10 feet.

Size: Up to a length of 16 inches.

Diet: Bivalves such as clams and oysters.

Misc.: Lightning Whelks are edible and support a small fishery.

Florida Horse Conch
Pleuroploca gigantea

Range: From the Carolinas to Florida and the Gulf of Mexico to Texas.

Habitat: Inhabits sand and soft bottom up to depths of 60 feet.

Size: Up to a length of over 20 inches and a weight of over 6 pounds.

Diet: Other mollusks.

Misc.: The Florida Horse Conch is the largest gastropod found in the waters of the United States. It is the state shell of Florida.

True Tulip
Fasciolaria tulipa

Range: From the Carolinas to Florida and around the Gulf of Mexico to Texas. Also found in the Caribbean.

Habitat: Inhabits sand, soft bottom, and seagrass up to depths of 30 feet.

Size: Up to a length of 9 inches.

Diet: Other mollusks.

Misc.: There is a similar and smaller species called the Banded Tulip *(Fasciolaria lilium)*.

Florida Cerith
Cerithium atratum

Range: From the Carolinas to Florida and the Gulf of Mexico to Brazil. Also found in the Caribbean.

Habitat: Inhabits structure, reefs, and sand bottom up to depths of 30 feet.

Size: Up to a length of 1.75 inches.

Diet: Algae.

Misc.: The Florida Cerith can be found in the aquarium trade.

Lettered Olive
Oliva sayana

Range: From the Carolinas to Florida and the Gulf of Mexico to Brazil.

Habitat: Inhabits sand bottom up to depths of 100 feet.

Size: Up to a length of 3 inches.

Diet: Scavenges and will also consume other mollusks.

Misc.: The Lettered Olive is a popular shell among collectors.

Giant Atlantic Cockle
Dinocardium robustum

Range: From the Carolinas to Florida and throughout the Gulf of Mexico to Central America. Also found in the Caribbean.

Habitat: Inhabits sand and soft bottom up to depths of 100 feet.

Size: Up to a length of over 5 inches.

Diet: Plankton that is filtered from the water.

Misc.: The Giant Atlantic Cockle sustains a small commercial fishery.

Calico Clam
Macrocallista maculata

Range: From the Carolinas to Florida and throughout the Gulf of Mexico to Brazil. Also found in the Caribbean.

Habitat: Inhabits sand bottom up to depths of 300 feet.

Size: Up to a length of 3.5 inches.

Diet: Plankton that is filtered from the water.

Misc.: The shell of the Calico Clam is popular among shell collectors.

Sunray Venus
Macrocallista nimbosa

Range: From the Carolinas to Florida and throughout the Gulf of Mexico to Brazil.

Habitat: Inhabits sand bottom up to depths of 25 feet.

Size: Up to a length of 6 inches.

Diet: Plankton that is filtered from the water.

Misc.: Attempts to develop a commercial fishery for the Sunray Venus have failed despite the clam being edible.

Green Mussel
Perna viridis

Range: Native to the South Pacific and Indian Oceans. Also found on the central west coast of Florida.

Habitat: Inhabits structure and reefs in shallow water.

Size: Up to a length of 6.5 inches.

Diet: Plankton that is filtered from the water.

Misc.: The Green Mussel is an exotic species that was first spotted in the Tampa Bay area in the late 1990's. It has the potential to create problems for native species.

Atlantic Wing Oyster
Pteria colymbus

Range: From the Carolinas to Florida and throughout the Gulf of Mexico to Brazil. Also found in the Caribbean.

Habitat: Inhabits structure, hard bottom, and reefs up to depths of 100 feet.

Size: Up to a length of 3.5 inches.

Diet: Plankton that is filtered from the water.

Misc.: The Atlantic Wing Oyster is commonly found attached to soft corals.

CNIDARIANS

Cnidarians are a group that contains invertebrates with many different shapes, sizes, and life histories. One of the defining characteristics of cnidarians are cnidocytes. Cnidocytes are specialized stinging cells. These cells are involved in the capture of prey. There are around 10,000 known species. These include corals, jellyfish, sea anemones, and hydroids. Cnidarians are found worldwide in all marine environments.

Christmas Tree Hydroid
Pennaria disticha

Range: From South Florida to the Gulf of Mexico. Also found in the Bahamas and the Caribbean.

Habitat: Inhabits structure and reefs up to depths of 60 feet.

Size: Up to a height of 4 inches.

Diet: Plankton that is captured by its tentacles.

Misc.: The Christmas Tree Hydroid is an exotic species in Hawaii.

Yellow Sea Whip
Pterogorgia citrina

Range: Atlantic and Gulf coast of South Florida and throughout the Caribbean. Also found in the Bahamas.

Habitat: Inhabits reefs and hard bottom up to depths of 40 feet.

Size: Colony up to a height of 12 inches.

Diet: Plankton that is captured by its tentacles.

Misc.: The Yellow Sea Whip can be found in several colors such as yellow, green, and purple.

Sea Whip
Leptogorgia virgulata

Range: From the Northeastern U.S. to Florida and throughout the Gulf of Mexico to Brazil.

Habitat: Inhabits structure, reefs, and hard bottom up to depths of 60 feet.

Size: Colony up to a height of 1.5 feet.

Diet: Plankton that is captured by its tentacles.

Misc.: The Sea Whip can be found in several colors such as red, yellow, orange, and purple. It can be found in low salinity waters.

Regal Sea Fan
Leptogorgia hebes

Range: From the Carolinas to Florida and throughout the Gulf of Mexico to Brazil.

Habitat: Inhabits structure and reefs up to depths of over 100 feet.

Size: Colony up to a height of 1.5 feet.

Diet: Plankton that is captured by its tentacles.

Misc.: The Regal Sea Fan can be found in several colors such as red, yellow, orange, and purple.

Snowflake Coral
Carijoa riisei

Range: From Florida to Brazil. Also found in the Caribbean.

Habitat: Inhabits structure and reefs up to depths of 180 feet.

Size: Colony up to a height of 10 inches.

Diet: Plankton that is captured by its tentacles.

Misc.: The Snowflake Coral has spread beyond its native range and is now found in Indo-Pacific waters.

Elliptical Star Coral
Dichocoenia stokesii

Range: From both coasts of South Florida and the southern Gulf of Mexico to northern South America. Also found in the Bahamas and the Caribbean.

Habitat: Inhabits structure and reefs up to depths of over 200 feet.

Size: Colony up to a width of 15 inches.

Diet: Plankton that is captured by its tentacles.

Misc.: Fossils of the Elliptical Star Coral have been found that date back to the Eocene Epoch (56 - 34 million years).

SPONGES

Sponges are the simplest of multi-cellular animals. They have no organs or nervous, respiratory, and circulatory systems. The fossil record for sponges dates back over 500 million years. Some of the oldest animal fossils found are those of sponges. There are over 5,000 known species. Adult sponges spend their lives attached to the substrate where they filter nutrients out of the water. There was once an important commercial fishery for certain species. The fishery has been greatly reduced due to the advent of the synthetic sponge.

Loggerhead Sponge
Spheciospongia vesparium

Range: Atlantic and Gulf coast of South Florida. Also found in the Caribbean.

Habitat: Inhabits reefs, hard bottom, and seagrass up to depths of 60 feet.

Size: Up to a width of 5 feet.

Diet: Organic matter that is filtered from the water.

Misc.: Many species of invertebrates reside in the internal canals of the Loggerhead Sponge.

Stinker Sponge
Ircinia felix

Range: Atlantic and Gulf coast of South Florida. Also found in the Bahamas and the Caribbean.

Habitat: Inhabits structure, reefs, and seagrass up to depths of 60 feet.

Size: Up to a width of 12 inches.

Diet: Organic matter that is filtered from the water.

Misc.: The Stinker Sponge gets its name due to the foul odor it emits when taken out of the water.

Orange Ball Sponge
Cinachyra kuekenthali

Range: From the Carolinas to Florida and throughout the Gulf of Mexico to Brazil. Also found in the Bahamas and the Caribbean.

Habitat: Inhabits structure and reefs up to depths of 300 feet.

Size: Up to a width of 8 inches.

Diet: Organic matter that is filtered from the water.

Misc.: The surface of the Orange Ball Sponge may sometimes look brownish due to algal growth.

Orange Lumpy Encrusting Sponge
Ulosa ruetzleri

Range: Atlantic and Gulf coast of Florida. Also found in the Bahamas and the Caribbean.

Habitat: Inhabits structure and reefs up to depths of 75 feet.

Size: Up to a width of 12 inches.

Diet: Organic matter that is filtered from the water.

Misc.: The Orange Lumpy Encrusting Sponge is a very common species in its range.

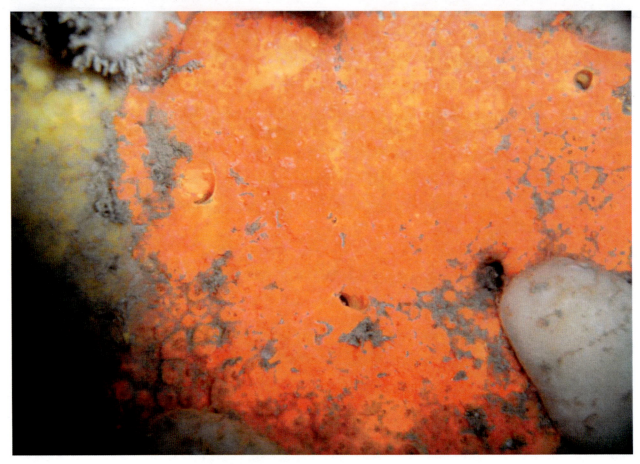

Red Boring Sponge
Cliona delitrix

Range: From South Florida to throughout the Gulf of Mexico. Also found in the Bahamas and the Caribbean.

Habitat: Inhabits structure and reefs up to depths of 100 feet.

Size: Up to a width of 3 feet.

Diet: Organic matter that is filtered from the water.

Misc.: The Red Boring Sponge will often kill the coral that it is growing on.

Chicken Liver Sponge
Chondrilla nucula

Range: Atlantic and Gulf coast of South Florida and throughout the Caribbean.

Habitat: Inhabits structure and reefs up to depths of 20 feet.

Size: Up to a width of 4 inches.

Diet: Organic matter that is filtered from the water.

Misc.: The Chicken Liver Sponge contains a toxin that helps prevent predation by other animals.

ALGAE

Algae are photosynthetic organisms. There are three kinds of algae. These are the green, red, and brown algae. Despite the resemblance to plants, algae are generally classified as protists. Green algae are sometimes grouped with plants. The fossil record for algae dates back around 3 billion years. It is from algae that terrestrial plants evolved. Kelp, a type of brown algae, can grow over a foot a day and reach a height of over 100 feet.

Green Grape Alga
Caulerpa racemosa

Range: From Florida south to Brazil. Also found in Bermuda and the Caribbean.

Habitat: Inhabits reefs up to depths of over 300 feet.

Size: Up to a height of 12 inches.

Diet: Photosynthetic.

Misc.: Green Grape Alga is found in the aquarium trade.

Fuzzy Finger Alga
Dasycladus vermicularis

Range: Has a worldwide distribution.

Habitat: Inhabits structure and reefs up to depths of 25 feet.

Size: Up to a height of 2.5 inches.

Diet: Photosynthetic.

Misc.: The Fuzzy Finger Alga is being utilized in the research of underwater adhesives.

Red Sea Lettuce
Halymenia floridana

Range: South Atlantic coast of the U.S. to Florida and throughout the Gulf of Mexico to Brazil.

Habitat: Inhabits reefs and hard bottom up to depths of 140 feet.

Size: Up to a length of over 12 inches.

Diet: Photosynthetic.

Misc.: The Red Sea Lettuce may be attached to the substrate or drifting.

White Scroll Alga
Padina jamaicensis

Range: Atlantic and Gulf coast of South Florida. Also found in the Bahamas and the Caribbean.

Habitat: Inhabits reefs and hard bottom up to depths of 50 feet.

Size: Up to a height of 6 inches.

Diet: Photosynthetic.

Misc.:   The White Scroll Alga is a brown alga.

Species Seen

1 _____
2 _____
3 _____
4 _____
5 _____
6 _____
7 _____
8 _____
9 _____
10 _____
11 _____
12 _____
13 _____
14 _____
15 _____
16 _____
17 _____
18 _____
19 _____
20 _____
21 _____
22 _____
23 _____
24 _____
25 _____
26 _____
27 _____
28 _____
29 _____
30 _____
31 _____
32 _____
33 _____
34 _____
35 _____
36 _____
37 _____
38 _____
39 _____
40 _____

41 _____
42 _____
43 _____
44 _____
45 _____
46 _____
47 _____
48 _____
49 _____
50 _____
51 _____
52 _____
53 _____
54 _____
55 _____
56 _____
57 _____

58 _____
59 _____
60 _____
61 _____
62 _____
63 _____
64 _____
65 _____
66 _____
67 _____
68 _____
69 _____
70 _____
71 _____
72 _____
73 _____
74 _____

Made in United States
Orlando, FL
30 September 2023